To Be Opened Before Christmas

This is one Christmas gift you may open before Christmas . . . For it is a friendly gift that is meant to be shared: a greeting, a remembrance, a gift of warmth and tenderness, of human faith and generosity.

These vignettes, written with a poet's gift of grace and insight, capturing each year some thought of Christmas for a more lasting record, have bridged both time and distance. Written to her friends, far distant from where at Christmas she might find herself, they have already had a distribution far beyond the circle to which Frances Parkinson Keyes, the beloved author, addressed them.

In gathering them here this Christmas season, the publisher hopes to include you among the friends of Mrs. Keyes who, each year for many years have received from her, through the mails, her familiar envelope, and have not waited until Christmas to open it and let her words warm their hearts.

A HAWTHORN BOOK

FRANCES PARKINSON KEYES'

Christmas Gift

FRANCES PARKINSON KEYES'

Christmas Gift

Illustrations by Tracey Penton

HAWTHORN BOOKS, INC.

Publishers • New York

First Edition, November, 1959

ACKNOWLEDGMENTS

The author gratefully acknowledges the kind permission of *The Chicago Tribune* for permission to reprint "Chris'mus Gif'!" which was issued in that paper's special Christmas issue of Dec. 3, 1944 under the title of "Great Gifts Live in the Heart at Christmas," and the permission of the *National Catholic Welfare Conference News Service,* Washington, D.C., which used "Our Lord Had a Grandmother, Too." *This Week Magazine* is gratefully thanked for permission to reprint parts of "Anniversary" which appeared July 10, 1949 and from which was adopted "The Virgin of Vieux." The quotation in "Keeping Christmas" is taken from *The Devil's Brood* by Alfred Duggan, published by Coward-McCann, Inc., © 1957 by Alfred Duggan, and was used by special permission.

Foreword

A NUMBER OF YEARS AGO, I BEGAN TO REALIZE that I might completely lose touch with my oldest and dearest friends if I did not see them, or at least communicate with them more frequently. I could not change my way of life: I had to travel a great deal because of my work, and even when I was not moving rapidly from place to place I was obliged to spend long periods—also because of my work—away from Virginia, New England and Washington, D.C., which represent my natural centers for close ties of friendship and kinship. It was then that I hit upon a plan, which, though not altogether satisfactory, was at least better than nothing: every year, at Christmastime, I would write a short verse or article, appropriately illustrated, which would carry a message that would, or should, have fairly general appeal. I would have this printed on a four-page folder, but I would limit it in length, so that the illustrations and

5

the printed text would not cover more than three pages. The last page I would reserve for a personal, handwritten note; that much, at any rate, I could achieve once a year, if not oftener.

The results of this compromise with extensive correspondence have been surprising. The requisite number of cards leaped from a few hundred to a thousand and we were soon often hard put to find remainders when persons asked for extra copies, either for themselves or for friends. Several of the little articles were reprinted, wholly or in part, in newspapers, or were made the subject of editorials; and one—"Our Lord Had a Grandmother, Too"—resulted not only in wide syndication, as it was originally written, but in a book, where the text was, of course, greatly expanded to include a complete biography of St. Anne. Eventually, the suggestion that these Christmas cards—for I had never considered them anything more important than that—should be gathered together in book form, came from two persons whose judgment I greatly respect, both personally and professionally: Isabel Kinnear Griffin, who, with her husband Bulkley, heads one of the outstanding news bureaus in Washington, D.C., and Edward J. Gallagher, owner and publisher of the *Laconia (N.H.) Evening Citizen,* which is outstanding among the daily newspapers of the smaller American cities. Still, probably nothing would have come from their suggestions if I had not happened to mention them to Mr. K. S. Giniger, of Hawthorn Books. Mr. Giniger had flown to New Orleans to see me about an assignment entirely unrelated to Christmas cards, but, in the course of conversation, he happened to mention Bob Considine's *Christmas Stocking,* which he had brought out last year. I suddenly bethought me of what Isabel Griffin and Edward Gallagher had said and mentioned it to him. With the swiftness which, apparently, is characteristic of Mr. Giniger, he asked if he could see some of these cards. From the storage place of the still unsettled office—for we had only just returned to New Orleans after a six months' absence—we gathered as many remainders as we could find, cooperative friends supplied us with a few more, and the result is this little book. I hope it will mean as much to the general public as its separate parts have evidently meant to their recipients.

FRANCES PARKINSON KEYES
Beauregard House,
New Orleans, La.

Contents

FOREWORD • 9

"Chris'mus Gif'!" • 13

The Gift of the Past • 17

The Gift of Speech • 21

Keeping Christmas • 27

Two Poems for Christmas: • 35

My Library Fireplace • 35

Figures on My Desk • 38

Our Lord Had a Grandmother, Too • 41

A Gift from Spain • 47

The Gift of Song • 55

The Virgin of Vieux • 63

Our Lady of the Bayous • 71

Home for Christmas • 81

Follow a Star • 87

THE AUTHOR AND HER BOOK

FRANCES PARKINSON KEYES'

Christmas Gift

"Chris'mus Gif'!"

*. . . The first words I heard,
on Christmas morning, were
"Chris'mus Gif'!"*

WHEN I WENT TO LIVE AT THE COTTAGE, A plantation house on the River Road in Louisiana, the first words I heard, on Christmas morning, were "Chris'mus Gif'!" Creacy, my maid, said it when she brought my breakfast tray, decorated with one of the red camellias from my garden. King, the gardener, said it when I went to the garden myself, to gather more camellias with which to decorate the dinner table. Jack, the handyman, said it when I stepped onto the front gallery to see if it were swept against the coming of my guests. And, before the

13

day was over, Jack's quiverful of pickaninnies—nine
of them in all, without counting the baby, who was
still too young to say it!—found an excuse for coming to the Big House and calling out, "Chris'mus
Gif'!"

I was glad I had something for each and all of
them tucked away already. They gave me a new
feeling about Christmas. The savory dinner cooking
in the kitchen, the great tree standing at the end of
the hall, the quaint crêche in the parlor fireplace—all
these were associated with lifelong habits of celebration. But it was not until I went to live on a Louisiana plantation that dusky servitors surrounded me,
confident that they would have only to ask in order
to receive. They made me more conscious of the gifts
I had myself than I had ever been before.

I have the gift of work. I am doing work that I
love, in surroundings that I have chosen, and I have
the assurance that it is going well. For a long time,
my tasks were hard and thankless. Nothing about
them suggested a benefit received. All that is different now.

I have the gift of health. For many years I was an
invalid, for many others a cripple. Now, though still
very lame, I am otherwise well.

I have the gift of companionship. I am far from
my family, or perhaps I should say my family is far

from me. Two of my sons live in New England, the third in New York. It is not always possible for them to leave their work long enough to come to Louisiana or for me to leave mine long enough to go North; and then, there is the troop of grandchildren, each with individual interests, which must also be considered. When we can get together, it is a time of great rejoicing; but, when we cannot, we do not repine.

Most of my old friends are in the North, too. But I have found new friends. They call me "Aunt Frances" if they are younger than I am, and "Cousin Frances" if they are my own age. This does not entail any of the usual obligations of relationship. It merely means that they do not think of me as a damn-yankee. It is very pleasant.

I have the gift of faith: faith in myself, long lost; faith in humanity, long shattered; faith in the future, long dark; faith in God, omnipresent. I think faith is the greatest gift of all, unless it be courage, and having the first, who can lack the second? Certainly not I. Like Creacy and King, Jack and all his picka-ninnies, I have asked and received. I hope that you have, too.

"Chris'mus Gif'!"

—The Cottage, River Road,
near Baton Rouge, La.

*
* *
* 15 *
* *
*

The Gift of the Past

In Normandy, during the
Christmas holidays . . .

THERE IS MIDNIGHT MASS IN THE VILLAGE
churches, with all the *charitons*—those men of
good will and good standing in the community,
pledged to alleviate suffering and sorrow—stationed
in the choir stalls, holding their great staves up-
right, and wearing the vestlike crimson and gold
chaprons reserved for the greatest occasions. There
is a crêche beside the choir, not far from the statue
of the Little Sainte Thérèse, with small lights twin-
kling in front of it, and flickering over the figures
of Mary and Joseph and Jesus, of the Wise Men and

the shepherds. After Mass, there are *reveillons,* at château and cottage alike, with turkey—or maybe goose—served at two in the morning, instead of at two in the afternoon, as we would have it, but otherwise not so very differently after all.

Usually there is a *place du pauvre* at the festive board, and any forlorn stray, passing through the countryside, knows that if he knocks at the door of either château or cottage, he will be given a seat, and afterward a bed in the hay—at least, if he will promise not to listen to the animals who will begin to talk on the stroke of twelve. Such eavesdropping would bring bad luck to him and to his benefactors. But he does not doubt, and neither do they, that the cows and sheep will begin murmuring together at midnight and continue until dawn, for such is their privilege on Christmas Eve, because creatures of their kind once stood around the manger of the Christ Child.

Of course, there is also a Christmas tree, with presents on one side for the family and on the other for their faithful retainers. There are little shoes ranged around the chimney-piece for *Père Noël* to fill. And there is always carol singing, and a second *reveillon* on New Year's Eve.

It is a happy time for everyone, young and old, rich and poor, native son and stranger, and the memory of it lingers long after the merry-making is over.

It has been my great and proud privilege to have a share, more than once, in such celebrations and they have made a profound impression upon me. But how profound this was, I did not realize until I became acquainted with one at Malou, "a small proud château," near Lisieux, where I have been made especially welcome.

For more than five hundred years, in both peace and war, it has been the center for holiday celebrations like those I have tried to describe and has given them a significance that assures their survival and its own and that extends far beyond its own enduring walls. For Malou is no empty monument; it is a home, a haven, a stronghold, a pledge from the past to the future. And, as such, it has a universal meaning and a universal message—a meaning and a message as universal as the age-old greeting of

MERRY CHRISTMAS AND HAPPY NEW YEAR!

—*Malou, Norolles-par-Lixieux,
Calvados, France.*

*
*   *
*   19   *
*   *
*

The Gift of Speech

On Christmas Eve
At Midnight . . .

THERE IS A CHARMING OLD NORMAN TRADITION
to which many subscribe to this day, that on Christmas Eve, at midnight, all the farm animals are
granted the gift of speech until dawn, in blessed
memory of those who surrounded the manger at
Bethlehem. No one must go to the barns at this hour,
or even hover near by, where it would be possible to
overhear. The animals talk to each other, not to human beings. What they say is their own secret.

"Tradition, wisely controlled," the great Cardinal,
Merry del Val, has reminded us, "gives us manifest
proofs of the truths of our beliefs." I have found

this counsel almost invariably sound; and, on the strength of it, why should we not imagine that the animals which actually did surround the manger could also have talked to each other, and that they might even have had the gift of prophecy? To be sure, Mary and Joseph and the Christ Child would all have been in their stable and very soon the shepherds. But the animals would not have felt the same as they would about ordinary human beings today; they would not have minded speaking in the presence of the Holy Family and, anyway, they would have talked in their own language, so that what they said would still have been a secret, except to the Christ Child Himself Who, from the beginning, must have understood all tongues, just as He has always understood all hearts.

"It seems that three great kings are coming here from the East," the donkey might have said. "And they are going to bring magnificent gifts with them —gold and frankincense and myrrh—to this Baby, over Whom we have been watching ever since He was born. We feel that He is *Our* Baby. What a pity that we cannot offer Him gifts!"

"You have the great gifts of patience and endurance," the cow would have reminded him. "Early and late you carry heavy burdens over long distances, and never fall by the wayside or even falter and complain. It is rumored that the wicked King Herod has conceived the horrible idea of slaughtering the Innocents, and that the just man, Joseph, will be warned in a dream to take the young Child and His Mother and flee into Egypt. Joseph, a vigorous carpenter, can walk; but Our Baby and His Mother will need to ride. It would not surprise me if you were chosen to carry Them. What greater service could you render Him than to take Him to safety? Is that not better than a gift of gold?"

"Of course it is," the lamb might then have rejoined, "and looking further into the future, I believe He will choose you, rather than some noble charger, as His mount when He goes in triumph to Jerusalem and all the mighty throngs are spreading palms in His path and shouting, 'Blessed be the Kingdom of our Father David, that cometh in the name of the Lord. Hosannah in the highest!'"

A donkey is slow about most things and, therefore, might not immediately have answered his companions, the cow and the sheep. Nevertheless, he would have taken comfort in what they said and, finally, he would have spoken in his turn.

"You, too, shall serve Our Baby Who is also Our Lord," he would have said, turning to the cow. "I have heard that our Father David said, in one of the sweet songs which he sang, 'Out of Zion, the perfection of beauty, God has shined. Our God shall come and He shall not keep silence. He shall call upon the heavens from above . . . Hear My people and I shall speak . . . Gather My Saints together unto Me, those who have made a covenant with Me by sacrifice . . . Every beast of the forest is Mine and the cattle upon a thousand hills.' If the cattle were not of great value to Him, would David have sung of them at the same time he spoke of such things as the perfection of beauty and of Saints gathered together? Of course not! And when men speak of a land flowing with milk and honey, they mean a land of abundance. It is you who furnishes the milk. When you are sacrificed, you give your flesh. Even the hide which covers your body is of use to man. Wherefore not most of all to the Son of Man? The sandals which His cousin John will not feel worthy to unloose will be made of leather. You, too, have much to offer."

"But I," the sheep would have said meekly, "cannot carry burdens on my back and—"

"And do you think we can all serve in the same way?" inquired the cow, who, like the donkey, would be happier now than before and speak with some authority. "Your wool is used for garments— even for coats woven without a seam, such as Our Baby, Who is also Our Lord, shall one day wear when He goes to His death, which will be but the beginning of Eternal Life for Him and for all men. And you, even more than I, shall become a symbol of sacrifice. Among the names given Our Baby shall be yours—'the Lamb of God, Who taketh away the sins of the world.' And in days to come, Men shall pray to Him in this wise, adding, 'Grant us Thy peace.' If it had not been for the peace of the pastures, where the flocks feed, perhaps no one would ever think of wording a prayer in this way."

About this time, there would have been a knock at the door and the shepherds would have asked to come in. As they entered the stable, the radiance of a star would have lightened its dimness, and its quietude would have been transfigured with the sound of distant music—the song of the angels. So the animals would have spoken no more. But all that they might have told each other was true and remains true until today.

I believe this is much the same story as the one on which the Normans founded their tradition, when they first began to believe that the animals in their stables talked to each other at the hour of midnight, on Christmas Eve. Of course, that is still their secret. But is there any reason why we should not believe it too?

—*The Oxbow, Newbury, Vermont.*

```
        *
     *     *
  *    25    *
     *     *
        *
```

Keeping Christmas

. . . More than a matter of churchgoing and exchanging presents . . .

A CHAPTER IN A RECENT BOOK* WHICH I HAVE greatly enjoyed begins like this:

"In 1170 the Old King planned to keep his Christmas in Normandy. At that time for a king to 'keep Christmas' was more than a matter of churchgoing and exchanging presents. At least since the days of William the Conqueror, probably from much earlier times, it had been the custom for the King of England to 'wear his crown' on the three great festivals

---

* See Acknowledgments.

*of the Christian year, Christmas, Easter and Pente-
cost. In strict theory every one of his tenants-in-chief
was supposed to attend the three annual crown wear-
ings . . . For these royal feasts there was special
ceremonial; though, like any other ceremonial which
involved the reading of the written formulae, it was
performed by clerks, it was in essence a lay function.
The choir of the chapel royal sang the anthem
Christus vincit, Christus regnat, Christus imperitas
as it was sung at a coronation . . . While his clerks
sang, the king went in procession from the chapel to
the great hall, to take his place on a throne at the
head of the table. Then all his courtiers and feudatories ate and drank sumptuously in his presence."*

I have found this passage both enlightening and
thought provoking. Not only do I visualize more
clearly than ever before the manner in which Christmas was celebrated by Henry II of England—the
monarch to whom reference is made as the Old
King, though in 1170 he was only thirty-eight!—and
his fellow ruler, Louis VII of France, who was also
the first husband of Henry's Queen, the gorgeous
and provocative Eleanor of Aquitaine; I also find
myself asking whether my own celebration of Christmas is "more than a matter of churchgoing and
exchanging presents." And I have come to the con-

clusion that though it is something more than that, it is not as much more as it ought to be.

Like the Christmas celebrations of those early Kings, it includes a dinner which if not actually "sumptuous" is certainly bountiful; and though no "courtiers and feudatories" are present at this feast, I generally have some and occasionally all of the members of my immediate family, which now numbers sixteen, around my laden table. We are all very happy together. But I have fallen away from the custom, once fairly general throughout New England in my childhood and scrupulously observed by my mother, of asking a few of our less fortunate friends to join us for this feast. In our Vermont village these were apt to be a lonely schoolteacher, a new minister who was only half acquainted with his flock, a young couple who were still not settled in their modest home, an elderly relative who was so vaguely a cousin that she was no one's real responsibility; in Boston it was people we had known in some other city or in Vermont: the country girl who had come to study music at the Conservatory, the country boy who was working his way through dental school, the Westerner who had decided the East was inhospitable, the Southerner who hated the chill winds that blew up Beacon Street and longed for the camellias blooming in his distant garden.

Such additions gave pleasure as well as received it; they added to the variety of our conversation, broadened our outlook, and deepened our consciousness that Christmas is a season of goodwill. When I keep Christmas this year, I hope I may again have guests to keep it with me who will do this for me.

And then, what about the friends who cannot actually be at my table? Of course, I send out some presents, I give a little money to church and charities; but how much time do I put in to selecting the gifts, how much self-sacrifice does the money represent? I am aware that in many countries there is no giving or receiving of presents at Christmastime; this is observed wholly as a religious festival, and the presents come later, on New Year's Day or Twelfth Night—Three Kings' Day—and after all the latter is especially appropriate, because it commemorates the Gifts of the Magi. But I have always thought that Christmas was appropriate too, for it commemorates God's gift of His only Son to the world and that was the greatest gift it has ever received; we do well to remind ourselves of that by our own evidences of generosity. But if the presents are only a matter of "exchange" they do not really mean very much. I shall try to remember that an elderly cousin is longing for a certain book which is out of print; I believe I know a firm which can

track it down for him. I shall try to remember that
a young grandson wants a ski sweater, and that the
further South I get the less likely I shall be able to
find one that is suitable; I must make that one of
my first purchases. A year's subscription to a leading newspaper will be especially welcome in one
quarter, a poinsettia plant in another. If I am too
busy or too thoughtless to remember such things, I
shall not be keeping Christmas as I should. And I
shall fail all the more lamentably if I do not begin
now, before Christmas comes any closer, to set aside
sums for those who not only want but need presents.
What I give may be only a drop in a bucket; but
buckets are filled with drops if there are enough of
these.

And then this matter of going to church. Yes, I
have always done that and I always shall. I believe
that any thoughtful Christian, whatever his form of
faith, who fails to make churchgoing part of his
Christmas celebration, misses much of its essential
meaning. So I am glad that from the tenderest age
I was taught to regard Christmas as a day for
churchgoing, as well as a day when my family and
my family's friends had a wonderful time together
and showered each other with presents. I hung up
my stocking before I went to sleep on Christmas
Eve, and woke in the cold darkness of Christmas

morning to find it bulging; I helped to decorate our big Christmas tree, and later found that, too, laden with presents as well as sparkling with lights. But the song of the angels was never drowned out by the sound of the sleighbells, nor was the radiant vision of the Christ Child obscured by the impersonation of a jolly Saint Nick. What is more, I was myself early taught, and early taught my children, to recite certain passages from the second Chapter of Saint Luke. And now I am asking myself if, for all my faithful churchgoing, I have kept those passages as close to my heart and my mind as I should have, if I am truly to keep Christmas. For it is not enough merely to go to Church. The Christmas crêche must be approached by us in the same way that the manger was approached by the shepherds. Do you remember?

And it came to pass, as the angels were gone away from them into heaven, the shepherds said one to another, Let us now go even unto Bethlehem, and see this thing which is come to pass, which the Lord hath made known unto us. And they came with haste, and found Mary, and Joseph, and the babe lying in a manger. And when they had seen it, they made known abroad the saying which was told them concerning this child. And all they that heard it wondered at those things which were told them by the shepherds. But Mary kept all these things, and pondered them in her heart.

We must not delay. We must "come with haste," if we are to find Mary, and Joseph, and the babe lying in the manger as soon as we need to. We must also make known the saying which has been told us concerning this Child. And we must ponder all these things in our hearts.

In that way we will keep Christmas the whole year 'round.

—*Sulgrave Club, Washington, D. C.*

Two Poems for Christmas

I

My Library Fireplace

*. . . So come and share
my hearth and home . . .*

My library fireplace is wide,
Its shining brasses glow;
The easy chairs on either side
Are comfortable and low.

Secure and strong the hearthstone lies
Beyond the deep-set grate,
And marble columns smoothly rise
To frame the hearth in state.

The mantel shelf is marble too,
A painting hangs above it—
If you should see my library, you,
Like me, would come to love it.

On rainy days and chilly days
The fire burns warm and bright,
And when the darkness falls, it plays
In lovely leaping light.

But once a year on Christmas Eve,
Script clear of logs and brasses,
It is made ready to receive
The little lambs and asses,

The quiet cows, the gentle sheep
That gather round a manger,
Where angels guard a Baby's sleep
And ward away all danger.

Bemused and meek St. Joseph stands
Near Wise Men from afar,
And Mary kneels, with folded hands,
Beneath a shining star.

And all the beauty, all the light
Embodied in the story

❦ *Christmas Gift* ❧

Of Christmas Eve is here, so bright,
The room reflects its glory.

So come and share my hearth and home
As often as you're able,
On gloomy days and cold—and come
To see my sacred stable,

Glad with the confidence that then
Together we'll receive
The blessing of Good Will to Men
That comes on Christmas Eve.

> —*Tradition,*
> *Alexandria, Va.*

II

Figures on My Desk

*Among the humdrum working
things . . . Some figurines
are placed.*

My study is my workshop too
And so my desk provides
Space for the tools I need to do
My writing; but besides,

Among the humdrum working things—
The pencils and the paste,

38

❧ *Christmas Gift* ❧

The pads, the shears, the clips, and strings—
Some figurines are placed.

Our Lady's framed by gilded rays
Which give her added glory.
(And when a weary writer prays
It helps to speed a story.)

Nearby a tiny crêche reveals
Our Lord's Nativity
(And when an earnest believer kneels
A Star is there to see.)

The statue came from Canada,
The crêche from Salvador.
(Folk build their shrines both near and far
But always to adore.)

I find a kinship with the men
Who carved those gilded rays,
And, through the crêche, within my ken
Comes Salvadorian ways.

And so through every working day
And every working night
I share the shrine at which I pray,
And find a guiding light.

For Mary and her little Son
A space is always clear—
And thus the Christmas benison
Prevails throughout the year.

—*The Quarters*
Beauregard House,
New Orleans, La.

40

Our Lord Had a Grandmother, Too—

"I still don't understand," the child said, "why they didn't go to Grandma's . . ."

NOT LONG AGO, I HAD THE PLEASANT EXPERIENCE of spending a considerable period in the agreeable city where I grew up, but from which, of late, I have unfortunately been absent much of the time. I greatly enjoyed every aspect of this homecoming, but most of all the experience of renewing old friendships, and of finding that nothing had happened to change or mar these. Some of my former schoolmates I had not seen in years; however, it was hard for me to believe there had ever been such a separation, when we were seated together around a cozy tea table close to an open fire—for the city in question is happily a place where cocktails have not wholly supplanted afternoon tea or central heating the hearthstone. On these occasions, congeniality seemed as complete and conversation as spontaneous and stimulating as ever; and in the course of one such reunion, a charming contemporary of mine related an incident which seemed to me especially touching.

"I was trying to tell my little granddaughter the story of the Nativity," this lady told us. "And the child kept saying, 'But I don't understand why Mary and Joseph had to go to a stable.' . . . 'Well, you see,' I repeated, 'there was no room for them at the inn. I said that before, darling. And they needed shelter. That's why they went to the stable.' The child looked more and more bewildered and she began to look troubled, too. 'I still don't understand,' she said again, and this time her voice trembled a little, 'Why didn't they go to Grandma's?' "

I have recalled this story many times since then, and each time it evokes several different thoughts. Of course I know that Joseph left Nazareth, where he plied his trade as a carpenter, and went to Bethlehem, the City of David, because "All went to be taxed, everyone into his own city" and Joseph was "of the House and lineage of David." It was probably requisite, and certainly natural, that "Mary, his espoused wife" should go with him. But I do not know why St. Anne did not go, too.

The Church teaches us that she and her husband, Joachim, like Joseph, belonged to the House of David, and, in this case, Bethlehem was her "own city" no less than his. But Scripture does not mention her, in this connection or any other; so perhaps it is not strange that I know very little about St. Anne, even though her cult is an old one. I realize that she was supremely favored because she was the mother of Mary and that she must have been worthy of this favor in the sight of God. I have been to the house in Nazareth which was hers and where the Annunciation took place—at least, according to tradition; I have also been to the shrine in Canada which is the scene of many miracles attributed to her, the authenticity of which I do not doubt. I have read that she is the Patroness of Brittany, whose most illustrious queen was her namesake, and that she is often "invoked by women in childbirth." And I have seen countless modern and rather mediocre statues representing her with her daughter, whom she is teaching to read. These statues, far from inspiring me, have always caused me to wonder why

the figure of St. Anne is so very tall in comparison
to the Virgin Mary's—a child old enough to read
is not so short that it does not reach its mother's
waist. To be sure, I have also seen a few wonderful
paintings of St. Anne by glorious old masters which
show her with the Virgin and Child and, usually,
with the little St. John as well; these have done a
great deal to offset the effect of the statues, both
because they are so beautiful in themselves and because they give the impression of a happy and united
family life, unshadowed by future sorrows—though
apparently she was already a widow, since St. Joachim never appears in them. But it was not until I
heard the puzzled child's query that I began to
visualize St. Anne primarily in her capacity of a
grandmother and to think of her with questioning
sympathy.

If she stayed at home in Nazareth when Mary,
who was "great with child," went to Bethlehem,
wasn't she very anxious about her daughter and
very eager to learn about the new baby? Did she
hear the "good tidings of great joy," if not directly
from the angels, then from some kindly neighbor
who came back to Nazareth before Mary and Joseph? Did the Star in the East shed its light far
enough for her to see? Did her first anxiety mount
to anguish when she learned about the Slaughter

of the Innocents? Was she very lonely while her
daughter was in Egypt? Did Jesus spend much time
with her in the little house where the angel had
announced His coming? Did she invite John to
stay there, too, so that the small cousins would be
company for each other? Was it she who taught
Jesus to read? Did she live long enough to see Him
"increase in wisdom and stature and in favor with
God and man?"

These are some of the questions which I ask myself about St. Anne, as I make my Christmas preparations. For I do so nowadays largely in my own
capacity as a grandmother; and I believe that no
one—not even the little child to whom the Christmas
celebration is still his most thrilling experience—
has greater cause for rejoicing on this day of days
than the mature woman to whom the revelation
of the Nativity seems more wonderful every year. I
say this with the realization that I am singularly
favored because I usually have some of my large
family with me (twice within the last decade, we
have *all* been together, converging from various distant points in both North and South America), and
because, this year, the birth of twin girls, within the
Christmas cycle, has given me, as their grandmother,
an added cause for joy. But I also say it with the
blessed knowledge that the most seemingly solitary

Christmas need never be lonely for me—or for any other human being—to whom the Child of Bethlehem has become "a living bright reality."

He must have been very real to St. Anne, even if she was alone in Nazareth when He was born in Bethlehem. I do not doubt that she can make Him very real to all of us, on His birthday, if we ask for this grace with trustful and humble hearts.

—*Beauregard House,*
New Orleans, La.

46

A Gift from Spain

*"Take this with you,
Señora," he said . . .*

NEARLY ALL THE MEMORIES OF MY RECENT STAY
in Spain are permeated with its sunshine and its
splendors. Not a day passes unbrightened by grateful recollections of some marvel that I visited or
revisited: the cathedral at Tarragona, its rose-colored
façade bathed in the lambency of late afternoon.
The aqueduct at Segovia, towering four-tiered above
a busy square and curving, in majestic length, out
toward the plains. The fountains at La Granja, soar-
ing and sparkling, and the quiet pools beneath them
transfigured by their image. The serpentine walls of
Avila, inclosing a city which some have called stern,

but which, to me, seemed the abode of glory. The magnificent treasures of art which the Duke of Alba has salvaged from the ruins of revolution, and gathered together in simple surroundings, awaiting the time when they can be restored to their rightful place in the Liria Palace, now happily under repair. The verdant, rolling landscape, unbroken on every side until it reaches the horizon, which surrounds the Royal Country Club near Madrid. . . .

And not all my grateful memories are centered on monuments and marvels. They linger also on lunch at the *albergue* in Benicarló and on supper at the Hosteria del Estudiante at Alcalá de Henares —the first on a flower-rimmed terrace, facing the sea, the second in a high-raftered room, leading into a cloistered courtyard. They linger on the cliffs above the beach at Javea, on the pottery factories at Manises, on the tiled street signs at Sitges, on the *bodegas* and geranium-covered walls at Puerta de Santa María. They linger on the collections of such noted *couturiers* as Pertegaz and Pedro Rodriguez, on the Spanish silks and Spanish laces of which their creations are fashioned. Yet, if in the midst of all this reminiscent musing, I were suddenly asked the question, "But in which one place, of all others, are the greatest number of your wonderful memories centered?" I should have to answer, "In Valencia."

Perhaps one reason for this is that the approach to it, through rich rice fields and fragrant orange groves, in the cool of the evening, seemed so doubly beautiful after long stretches of barren land, seen in the burning noonday—first impressions are often lasting impressions. Perhaps another reason is that I attended a meeting of the Tribunal of the Waters, that unique court, comprising eight countrymen, which, uninterruptedly for nearly a thousand years, has met every Thursday outside the main doorway of the cathedral to pass on all problems pertaining to the *huerta,* or irrigated land, which surrounds Valencia and makes it a city of fertility—and that this institution seemed to me the most wholly democratic that I have ever seen in action. Perhaps still another reason is that I was able to visit a variety of splendid and significant buildings without haste and under expert guidance—the local Parliament Building, where the ceilings are bright with the first gold that came from the New World, and the old Silk Exchange, where the columns of twisted marble rise to a vaulted ceiling of imperishable grandeur. Again, perhaps it is the simpler things which are responsible for this feeling—the peasants coming in from the country with hand-woven, hand-embroidered linen to sell, and the gay flower market and the charming regional costumes and the great foaming pitchers of orange juice and the *paellas* of rice and sea food, sizzling in their iron skillets.

All these are memorable, each in its own way, and it is hard to decide which is the most important among them or which is most securely enshrined in my heart. Yet, if someone suddenly said to me, "Very well. I accept your statement that more of your happy memories are centered in Valencia than in any other one place. But which, among those in Valencia, means the most to you?" I should have to say, "Its hospitality."

My own country people, the members of our Consular Staff, were hospitable to me. The nationals of other countries, whose professions have brought them to Valencia, were hospitable to me. The Spaniards themselves were hospitable to me. This hospitality took many different forms, from a glass of sherry or a cup of tea to a six-course dinner, in many different places—clubs, country houses, city apartments. And finally, it took the form of an audience in the Palace of the Archbishop, His Excellency, Marcelino Olaechea Loizaga.

He received me in a great room where the walls were lined with crimson brocade and the massive furniture was elaborately carved. Yet the atmosphere of this vast apartment was not oppressive, as I have sometimes found that of similar places to

be, and its ornaments were not gloomy or gory in
character, as is also sometimes the case as far as the
painting and statuary of clerical abodes are con-
cerned. Indeed, the ornament which most arrested
my attention was a silver statuette not more than two
feet high which stood on a table near the doorway—
a statuette modeled after the famous *Virgen de Los
Desamparados,* which is the object of such venera-
tion in Valencia.

I found myself glancing toward it, frequently, in
the course of conversation. Indeed, it was hard to
keep my eyes off it. But I was very careful not to
voice this admiration; in a Spanish house, from the
highest to the lowest, this is a dangerous thing to do,
for Spanish courtesy demands that your host then
offer you the object of your admiration. Nevertheless,
in spite of my care, the Archbishop must have di-
vined the irresistible attraction it had for me—because, as I was saying goodbye and we neared the
doorway, he paused in front of the statuette and
then held it out to me.

"Please take this with you, *Señora,*" he said. And,
as I tried to exclaim in protest, he silenced me by
raising his free hand, the one on which the great
ecclesiastical ring glittered. "You should not hesi-
tate to accept it," he told me, speaking in a voice of
kindly authority. "You will give it a place of honor,

I am sure, and it will make me very happy to think
that this silver statuette, which is so completely
Spanish, has been enshrined in an American home.
It will not only be a symbol of the faith we share. It
will be a symbol of the bond between your country
and mine. Now I will give you my blessing. Go with
God."

So I accepted the little silver statue, and it now
stands, as it did in Spain, on a flower-banked table,
while awaiting a more permanent place, peacefully
presiding over the turmoil of holiday preparations.
In my house there will also be a tree glowing with
lights from Christmas Eve until Twelfth Night,
stockings hung by the fireplace under a garlanded
mantel, wreaths bright with ribbons at the doors
and windows, yaupon berries in the tall vases, poinsettia plants, both red and white, on the newel posts
of the stairway and the flower stands of the porch,
ruby-colored glass on the dining-room table. Pack-
ages wrapped in gay papers and tied with tinsel rib-
bon will mount higher and higher around the tree;
and after Midnight Mass, when everyone else is
sound asleep, the matriarch of the family will check
to see that Santa Claus has done his duty and that
every stocking is bulging. Presently, stealing in from
the kitchen, will come the scents which presage
chicken pie for breakfast, according to unbreakable

tradition of the household; and later, those of turkey and "all the fixin's" for family dinner, of coffee and eggnog and fruit cake and beaten biscuit filled with ham for guests at all hours. And, in the midst of these sights and scents of an American Christmas, the Virgin from Valencia will be enshrined—a symbol of shared faith and of a bond between two countries which was already strong before the Pilgrims landed on Plymouth Rock and the Cavaliers settled Virginia: a visible reminder of all that a great poet— Katrina Trask—meant when she wrote:

"Kings have waged warfare, armies lost and won,
Tyrants their battle bolts long years have hurled;
But lo! The Virgin and her little Son
Still rule the world."

—*Pine Grove Farm,*
North Haverhill, N. H.

*
*   *
*   53   *
*   *
*

The Gift of Song

*God gave us memories so that we
could have roses in December.*

THERE IS AN OLD SAYING I HAVE ALWAYS LOVED
to the effect that God gave us memories so that we
could have roses in December. This is meant figura-
tively, of course, and that is the way I take it—I cannot very well take it literally, for I am fortunate
enough to spend my winters in a region where I have
only to step into my own garden to gather the roses
for my desk! It is also true that I have not yet quite
reached the December of life; but this period is already near enough for me to find the evenings that I
spend quietly knitting, with my dog Lucky beside
me, rewarding rather than monotonous. Moreover,

the main reason that they are thus rewarding is because I am companioned, not only by Lucky, but by memories—some of the distant past, some of the months that lie immediately behind me, some of the two interwoven. For instance:

It was my custom, when my children were little, to spend at least an hour reading aloud to them before their early bedtime, and then listen to their prayers. When they were finally tucked in, I lay down beside them and sang two or three hymns before we parted for the night. (Apparently, the memory of this custom has not faded from my sons' consciousness, either, for not too long ago one of them sent me a poem entitled *Songs in the Night*, which lauds the "brave old hymns, a shining host . . . my mother used to sing.") Some of the hymns were chosen almost haphazardly to begin with and afterward sung over and over again, because they proved to have a special appeal; others were selected because they were peculiarly appropriate for a certain occasion or a certain season. There were favorites among these, too. The one which I was most often asked to sing, at Christmastime, began:

> *Once in royal David's city*
> *Stood a lowly cattle shed,*

Where a mother laid her baby,
In a manger for his bed;
Mary was that mother mild,
Jesus Christ her little child.

I had not thought of this hymn for years. But so
spontaneously that I could not suppress the impulse,
I found myself singing it again, under my breath, as
I sat last summer on my balcony of the King David
Hotel in Jerusalem, looking out across its splendid
gardens toward the new city in the foreground and
the old city rising beyond it. Thus seen, the dividing
line between the two parts disappears completely;
and the consciousness of present-day conflict, and
the inevitable tragedies which accompany it, is sub-
merged in a sense of Biblical reawakening.

Years ago, when I first visited what we then called
the Holy Land, I was told that I was doomed to certain disillusionment. Dreading this, I echoed the
petition which came to me from an unknown source:

Lord Jesus, make Thyself to me
A living bright reality.

The prayer was prodigally answered then. From
the moment of my arrival, on Ascension Day, when

I went straight to a sunrise service on the Mount of Olives, throughout the long weeks when I visited every locality connected with the history of Our Lord, the "living bright reality" was with me day and night. I had not one moment of disillusionment.

This time, however, I feared it would be different. I could not help recognizing the element of tenseness in the Middle East; probably I would not have gone there except for the insistence of my publisher, who felt that the book on St. Anne which I was writing might lack authenticity unless I visited the scenes connected with her life: not only the village of Nazareth, where she spent so much time, but also the church on the site of her urban home, near the Golden Gate and the Pool of Bethesda, and the encircling garden where, sitting beneath a laurel tree, she bemoaned her childlessness—yet lived to teach her daughter, and probably her Grandson as well, while sheltered by its pleasant shade. I believe it is just such a secluded spot as this that the hymnist must have had in mind when, in writing, *O Mother dear, Jerusalem,* he worded one verse:

> *Thy gardens and thy goodly walks*
> *Continually are green,*
> *Where grow such sweet and pleasant flowers*
> *As nowhere else are seen.*

58

It also seems logical that, as he saw more and more of the city, he was moved to continue:

> *Right through thy streets, with silver sound,*
> *The living waters flow,*
> *And on the banks, on either side,*
> *The trees of life do grow.*

At all events, from the time I went to St. Anne's home, my research brought me increasingly rich rewards. As has been rightly said, she is "the bridge between the Old Law and the New Testament," for she was the direct descendant of David—and also the grandmother of Jesus. While I pursued my study of her life, it was not only her Grandson who again became a "living bright reality" to me; the connection between the great kings and heroes of the Old Testament and the shepherds and soldiers and saints of the New seemed much closer than ever before; and all ceased to be dim and distant figures. They were so vital that I could almost hear the messages that have come echoing down from them through the ages, almost see them as I sat looking down on their streets. Truly,

> *Apostles, martyrs, prophets there,*
> *Around my Saviour stand. . . .*

There is the throne of David;
And there, from care released,
The shout of them that triumph,
The song of them that feast.

In such a setting, none of us needs to delve into the past; the past comes rushing out to meet us. All we have to do is to await—and accept—the vision of those who once lived there in the flesh and who have left us the record of what they said when they spoke with the tongues of men and of angels.

Of course, it is of not only "those brave old hymns," which I sang so long ago by my children's bedside, or of the new significance that they have for me, that I think as I sit so quietly knitting, now that another book is done, another journey ended, another Christmas close at hand. There are many other memories connected with my sons' childhood: the shared coasting in winter; the shared swimming in summer; the lessons we struggled through together; the long sieges of illness which were a still greater struggle. (Roses have thorns, even in December, else they would not be roses!) There are many other memories connected with my journeyings, especially the latest one: the morning at the old monastery in Daphni, near Athens, where I went to see

the superb eleventh century mosaics, depicting the
lives of St. Anne, the Virgin Mary and Our Lord; the
afternoon at Santa Maria Maggiore in Rome, where
I visited the manger, now so magnificently enshrined; the days and nights of work on an ocean
steamer, which plunged down, down, down and
then shuddered before it righted itself and clove its
way upward through the tempestuous waves of an
angry sea. And of course there are memories of
other Christmases, when I was not at home alone, as
I am now, but either far away or surrounded by an
ever-increasing family: the merry Christmas in San-
tiago when a group of Chilean friends shared my
eggnog with me, after Midnight Mass; the miserable
Christmas in France, when I lay abed with bronchial
pneumonia, discouraged and cold and lonely as well
as ill; the joyous Christmas in New Orleans when all
the children and grandchildren were with me, and
which inspired the holiday greeting, entitled "Our
Lord Had a Grandmother, Too," of which the current book is the outgrowth.

But still it is the memory of Jerusalem and of my
experiences there, nearly thirty years apart, which,
sooner or later, comes crowding to the forefront of
my consciousness. "It would be wonderful to know
that the inspiration for a message at the season of

good will could come once again from the city of David," a friend wrote me recently. I hope that all the friends I have included in this greeting will be glad that it has.

—*Compensation,*
Crowley, La.

The Virgin of Vieux

. . . a tower of strength.

QUITE NATURALLY, WE ALWAYS ASSOCIATE
Christmas with the birth of the Infant Jesus. But it
seems to me that, in so doing, we sometimes leave
the association incomplete. The story of the Nativity is not only the story of the Christ Child; it is
also the story of the angels who formed the multitudes of the heavenly host and of the shepherds who
watched their flocks by night. It is the story of a
star—and of a stable; of a royal Scion—and of a fulfilled prophecy. Even more, it is the story of a
carpenter's betrothed wife who became the Mother
of God's only begotten Son. Like many other birthday stories, it is not told in its entirety if it is con-

fined to rejoicing over a new-born baby, even though this Baby be the Prince of Peace and the Redeemer of the World; it must include a tribute to the Baby's Mother.

Because I feel so strongly that this is true, I also feel that Christmas is a fitting time to recall the story of the Virgin of Vieux.

Vieux is a small Norman village, not far from the proud city of Caen. It is well named, for it is very old indeed, and, during the days of the Roman Occupation, boasted carvings and colonnades, pretentious fountains, even an amphitheater. But gradually these glories crumbled away. In time, its beautiful little Romanesque church was its only outstanding landmark. A medieval statue of the Madonna and Child, surmounting a broken Roman column outside the apse, seemed symbolic of some supernatural power to survive a pagan empire.

Then came the Second World War, and, during the invasion of Normandy, a large portion of Our Lady's Church in Vieux was destroyed. Of course, this was only part of the general ruin. More than half the buildings in the village were demolished and many of the inhabitants were killed. The retreating Germans ordered the evacuation of the village and the survivors left it to find shelter where and as they could. A woman named Louise Houlbey was one of these refugees.

She did not feel she had much left to live for. She had long been a widow. Her married daughter, whose husband was already a prisoner in Germany, had been killed in the bombardment; because of the shells bursting over the churchyard, the officiating priest had felt obliged to limit the burial service to five minutes. Later that same day, twenty-seven neighbors of Louise Houlbey had been hastily buried in a common grave. Her home was one of the worst damaged; she had no hope of returning to it. She had no hope of anything.

But she had long been a mainstay to others and now she became a veritable tower of strength. She had managed to salvage two carts, and instead of guarding these for her own kin, she put them at the disposal of the oldest, the youngest and the worst wounded. To the rear of one cart she attached a wooden cage and thrust into it the poultry from her barnyard. Then, leading the other villagers, she struck sturdily out on foot and eventually found a temporary abiding place in a small village near Laval.

Almost immediately, she had a resurgence of faith in the future. As a young girl she had held a humble position at Fierville, a manor house near Vieux, and through frugality, aided by vision, had eventually saved enough to buy it. If it were still even partially intact, she could continue to count on its rental for revenue. Moreover, her own crops and those of her neighbors had been planted before the bombardment; there might still be a harvest. . . .

The evacuation had taken place between the tenth and thirteenth of July. Before the end of August, Louise Houlbey was back in Vieux and had taken up her temporary habitation in one of the less damaged farmhouses. Before October, every one of the surviving three hundred refugees had returned. They had long regarded Louise Houlbey as their leader and they now acted to recognize this leadership officially. They elected her their mayor and followed her into the fields, still strewn with mines, where they managed to salvage what remained of their harvest. It kept them alive through the winter.

A year later, the prisoners of war began to drift back. When the time came to plow and plant again, the acreage under cultivation was increased not only to provide food for the villagers, but also for the inhabitants of stricken Caen. And there arose the question of restoring the ruined church.

It was at this point that I first heard of Vieux, from André Noël, a Norman friend, who had close ties there. "Two or three million (francs) will be needed for rebuilding the destroyed nave," he wrote. "The funds of the Commune are insufficient for this even with some help from the State. Seven or eight hundred thousand (francs) at least will be required. Vieux has not been 'adopted' by any friendly foreign city; yet the famous Côte 112 was within the limits of the Commune and General Thomas declared that the seizure of this position marked the final point in the success of the Invasion and the beginning of the collapse of the German forces. Perhaps this fact, combined with the historic importance of Vieux, might move some of your influential friends to generosity. I know that you yourself are contributing to other great needs in France."

Most of my influential friends have so many calls upon their generosity that I hesitated to add to these; and it was true that I was already doing as much as I thought I could in another quarter. I sent a very modest check—twenty-five dollars, to be exact—and then I am afraid I forgot about Vieux temporarily. But when I was preparing to revisit France in the Autumn of '48, I wrote Monsieur Noël and asked him if it would be practical to visit Vieux. He replied that he and his wife would be delighted to go there with me and that the mayor, Madame Houlbey, had invited us to lunch.

The drive out from Caen did not take us more than half an hour. Then we drew up in the spacious though battered courtyard of a typical Norman farmhouse—gabled, half-timbered, solidly built. Our hostess came out to welcome us—a robust, elderly woman, her gray hair brushed simply back from her calm, intelligent face, her shabby black clothes worn with a dignity which precluded apology. She led the way into a raftered kitchen where a large table was spread with a white cloth. Luncheon would be just a plain meal, she told us; practically everything we were to eat had been raised on the farm. I had eaten "plain meals" in rural Normandy before and I knew that somehow she would have contrived to make this one delicious. After savoring it to the full, I asked her if she would not show me something of the surrounding countryside, adding that I should especially like to see Fierville and the ruined church.

I thought there was a mysterious quality in the smile with which she acquiesced. But we started out and soon I was gazing enthralled, first at the rolling fields, gilded with sunshine, and then at the flowers, massed in glowing colors against the stone battlements in the walled garden of Fierville. Coming back to the village by a different route, we rounded a curve, flanked on one side by an open *lavoir* and on the other by a neat block of freshly plastered houses. Then I saw a beautiful Romanesque church, surrounded by a cemetery bright with fresh blooms. I turned to Madame Houlbey in amazement.

"Why, I thought your church was in ruins!" I gasped.

"Pardon, madame. It *was* in ruins. We have rebuilt it."

"A *stone* church! With a *tiled* roof! But Monsieur Noël wrote me you did not have anywhere near enough money."

"That was a year and a half ago, madame. Afterwards you very kindly sent us a contribution."

"Twenty-five dollars! Less than eight thousand francs!"

"Yes, but that meant a great deal. It encouraged us to go ahead ourselves, knowing a friend in America was willing to help. Every member of the Municipal Council made a personal loan, to supplement the loan we received from the State and the general funds of the Commune. And we have done other things. Not much. But we have staged amateur theatricals and occasionally there has been a *carrousel.*"

"You mean to say that mine was your only outside contribution?"

"Yes, madame."

She went on talking quietly as we got out of the

car and walked along. When we came to the statue of the Madonna and Child, Madame Houlbey paused.

"This image was uninjured in the bombardment," she said. "I sought it out as soon as I returned to Vieux and found it here, intact. We have managed to keep it decorated with flowers from the beginning. Of course it was as necessary that we should rebuild Our Lady's sanctuary as it was that we should rebuild our homes. Surely that would be evident to anyone, madame."

"Yes," I said. I did not find it easy to talk. But I did add, "And if you hadn't come back to your ruins——"

"Then, of course, Our Lady could not have helped us. That too must be clear to anyone, madame."

This time I did not try to answer at all. But not a day has passed, since then, that I have not thought of Louise Houlbey and of the Virgin of Vieux—who so beautifully represents the Virgin of that first Christmas Eve so long ago, the Mother of the Saviour of the World.

—*Beauregard House,*
New Orleans, La.

＊
＊　　　＊
＊　　70　　＊
＊　　　＊
＊

Our Lady of the Bayous

You can go anywhere in the world from a bayou . . .

FRANCE HAS OUR LADY OF LOURDES, PORTUGAL
Our Lady of Fatima, Spain Our Lady of Montserrat,
Mexico Our Lady of Guadalupe; and each of these
favored countries has shared its blessings, divinely
derived, with the whole world, to its inestimable
benefit. But, as far as I know, Louisiana is the only
place where the title of Our Lady of the Bayous has
been bestowed on a shrine of the Blessed Mother,
nor has the story of how this came to pass been
widely told. It seems to me that Christmas of the
Marian Year is a wonderful time at which to tell it;
therefore, I will do so, as well as I am able.

I should not have heard about it myself, were it

not for Monsignor Fusilier, the pastor of St. Mary Magdalen Church in Abbeville. He was among the distinguished clerics who accompanied Bishop Jean-mard when the latter came to bless my newly acquired house in Crowley, "The Rice Capital of America"; afterward, graciously writing to tell me he had enjoyed this ceremony, he added that some French nuns had recently settled in the outskirts of Abbeville and that he hoped I would go to see them. Somehow, I gathered that these nuns were Benedictine refugees, like those who had settled in Bethlehem, Connecticut, and who inspired the beautiful film, "Come to the Manger." It seemed natural, if such were the case, that I should make a special effort to become acquainted with them and offer them such modest help as I could, because of my long and close associations with the Benedictines of Lisieux, and my knowledge of what the latter had lost and suffered during and after the war. If some destitute members of this Order had found refuge in my neighborhood, surely I should be among the first to welcome them.

It was with this in mind that I created the first possible opportunity of going to Abbeville; and, instead of Benedictines, I found Dominicans; instead of refugees, I found missionaries!

There were only three of them in the plain little

clapboarded house serving, at one and the same time, as convent, chapel and community center. As a matter of fact, I met only two of them then, as the third, Sister Jean Noël, a skilled *infirmière,* was helping out in the local hospital, which happened to be short handed. (I soon learned there was nothing exceptional about this small number; though the Priories of these *Dominicaines Missionaries des Campagnes*— Dominican Rural Missionaries—theoretically house six or eight Sisters, this number may be either reduced or increased, in accordance with existing laws of supply and demand, as long as it more or less follows a "family pattern.") The Superior, Sister Marie St. Paul, ushered me into the tiny guest room, placed a simple but delicious supper before me—I have since learned that she is no less skilled as a cook than as a musician—and explained the background, nature and *modus operandi* of the Apostolate she represented.

The foundation of these Rural Missionaries is, it seems, fairly recent—in fact, their foundress, Mère Marie de St. Jean, is still living, though she is already "revered as a saint" by her spiritual daughters. They operate on the premise that "a village is a little world. It has its own organization and mode of life. Everyone knows everyone else. Mother Church becomes an integral part of such a center. She brings individuals and families close to her, so that the whole community may be infused with the essence of the Divine. Mingling with this village life, mindful of its temporal as well as its spiritual welfare, are our missionaries—sisters to everyone, loving everyone and by everyone loved."

It was with these ends and aims and convictions that the little group of three left the Motherhouse at Flavigny, near Dijon, and came to a section of Louisiana which is largely rural—indeed, the site of their first convent was, not so long ago, a cotton field. In talking with me, they could not say enough of the kindness and helpfulness with which they had been received; "Our district has about 1,500 families in it. Each family has its own little house, very restricted as to size, made entirely of wood, without attic or cellar.* Ours is exactly like those which surround it. Actually, it was made up of two little houses. One was in such a lamentable state that a volunteer worker doubted whether it could be transformed into anything serviceable. But good will and charity together wrought this miracle. In the course of a few months our little houses had been brought here from their original locations by truck, set up, joined, walled with clean clapboards,

---

* This type of construction is, of course, entirely different from that in France, as to both style and material; hence the emphasis upon it.

covered with a gray roof. And then, behold! Here were our cloistered cells, and our cross surmounting everything. The poor little shanty had become a pleasant convent. We could move in. And with what joy we did so, on the Feast of St. Rose of Lima!"

This story made a deep impression on me. I felt the simplicity of the nuns' equipment was extremely important; first, because actual habitation—and hence, actual service—could be achieved so much more quickly than with a more elaborate plant and second, because the obvious eagerness of the nuns to live on the same scale as the people among whom they had come to labor for could not help but strengthen the belief that they were sincere. Certainly the results they achieved seemed to indicate the inspired wisdom of their ways. A scant week after the Sisters took possession, the first Mass was celebrated in their little chapel. "The chapel was very simple. The walls, the altar, the Communion rail, the kneeling benches, were all of plain matching wood. But the sculptured figure of Christ stood out in solemnity and beauty. We were surrounded by our friends, both white and colored. We would have been sorry, on such a day, not to see the two separate parishes represented; but our colored friends were invited by the white ladies themselves, and we were present at the Holy Sacrifice as children of the same

Father. All our friends seemed happy and we were deeply moved. The atmosphere was calm and rapt. Our Lady had watched over us and brought everything to a happy outcome, as she always does."

Our Lady? Yes, of course. But Our Lady in what guise? Not the *Morena* in the miraculous painting at Guadalupe or the "Black Virgin" of Montserrat; not the "Beautiful Lady" of the grotto at Lourdes or the glistening white vision of the Portuguese children. Apparently, the missionary nuns were swift to realize this. I think they must have seen her as "calm and rapt" herself, a symbol of healing repose as well as unhurried progress and of ultimate and blessed achievement. She would not have been dressed in gray and green, since these are not her colors, but they are the ones that would have formed her background, for those are the colors of the slow-moving stream, which takes the place of a miraculous spring in this picture, and they are also the colors of the foliage; but there would have been bright flowers in the picture, too; and Our Lady's robe might well have been a soft yet radiant blue, like the sky above her.

At all events, this is what I gather from what Sister Marie St. Paul wrote the Motherhouse: "Why this strange name—'Our Lady of the Bayous?' Well, the bayous are the natural canals of the Mississippi.

76

They cover Louisiana with a network of wide brooks. Trawlers constantly go up and down our bayous, bringing fish and shrimp for our Friday dinner. There are many such streams, some with very picturesque names, and around here they are bordered by enormous live oaks with ghostly draperies of Spanish moss, by palm trees, banana trees and bamboo, and all about them are flowers. The bayous are themselves crossed and recrossed by artificial canals and finally by 'coulees' which lead the tiniest rivulets to the bayous. One passes close to our convent and, beyond the reeds, glides down to join the Bayou Vermilion." This is the place where the Sisters found rest and recreation. This, indubitably, was where they envisioned Our Lady of the Bayous.

Shortly after I came to Louisiana, a friend, wise in its ways, said to me, "You can go anywhere in the world from a bayou." He went on to explain that most of the passengers who took the riverboat from New Iberia to New Orleans, via Bayou Teche, had not started out in it, but from little places, on little bayous, in small luggers, even in pirogues. When these passengers reached New Orleans, they could go out across the Gulf and eventually reach any place they chose. I really did not need my friend's explanation to understand that he was trying to tell me anyone could make a great worldly success, in spite of small beginnings. But it was not until I heard about Our Lady of the Bayous I learned that, under her guidance, they could lead to spiritual success.

For the work of the missionary nuns has prospered, as it was bound to do. From the beginning, they showed themselves indeed "sisters to everyone, loving everyone and by everyone loved." They joined the Parent-Teacher Association and other lay organizations. They helped take the census. Soeur Jean Noël continued her faithful service at the hospital. Adults and children alike soon flocked to their community room. Four parochial choirs were formed. In time, no less than 350 children were coming to catechism classes and many were receiving liturgical instruction as well. More baptisms and more marriages in the Church took place. To celebrate their second Christmas, the nuns directed a *pastorale* in the sanctuary of the nearest church—a miracle play enacted by the children they had been teaching and who were permitted to bring their live lambs—a black one among the white, by the way!—to the Nativity scene. Presently, besides enlarging their activities at Abbeville, they acquired additional headquarters in an abandoned plantation house at Grosse Tête, some ninety miles distant, in a section having only four churches and three priests to minister to a population of 12,000, which is largely Catholic. Quite logically, this establishment has been named the Convent of the Epiphany—was it not after the birth of the Redeemer that the Wise Men came with their gifts? But it owes its being to the impetus given it by Our Lady of the Bayous, its inspiration to the tranquil retreat where the nuns found rest from their labors and refreshment for their souls by one of those quiet streams, bordered by beautiful trees, which descends without haste to the sea.

—*Compensation,*
Crowley, La.

*

*   *

*   79   *

*   *

*

Home for Christmas

*Every mother . . . may claim the
common bond of Motherhood
with Mary . . .*

I HAVE COME HOME FOR CHRISTMAS.

During a long absence, I have been seeing many
wonderful sights and doing many wonderful things
and meeting many wonderful people; but I have
been far from my own country and my own hearthstone and my own kith and kin. It seems inexpressi-
bly good to settle down among scenes long familiar,
to busy myself with the habitual duties of a house-
wife and to visit with my neighbors. The hot sug-
ared doughnuts that I eat for breakfast taste better
than any foreign food; the brown sitting room,

where the wallpaper has been unchanged for nearly one hundred and fifty years, and many of the furnishings, almost as old, has more charm for me than any baronial hall. From the window by the desk where I write without interruption, I look out on a countryside, now stripped of verdure, but infinitely restful to a weary traveler; it seems the very incarnation of stillness and serenity. When the day's work is done, I read from the same Bible and the same copy of Thomas à Kempis' *Imitation of Christ* from which my mother read every night and which have never been removed from the library desk. When I go to bed, I lie facing a fireplace where, when it would otherwise be cold, a friendly fire glows. Even after the rest of the room is dark, its flickering flames illumine the picture which hangs above the mantel. This picture is also the first thing I see when I wake in the morning. The name inscribed upon it is *The Holy Mother*.

It is not a valuable painting, merely an old engraving and, as far as I know, it is not the work of a famous artist. I have kept it over my bedroom mantel, instead of replacing it with something more notable, partly because it has hung there ever since I was a child and I have become attached to it, as I have to so many other things in this old house. But that is not the only reason. This picture is not merely a cherished possession; it is a reminder to me, as a mother, that every mother, however humble and obscure, may claim the common bond of Motherhood with Mary and insofar as lies within her power may, with God's help, glorify her estate in reverent imitation.

At this season the significance of the picture is enhanced; for it is also a reminder that Christmas is not only a children's day, as we are most prone to think of it; it is likewise a Mother's Day, in a sense far greater and more wonderful than any other day in the year, so designated, could ever possibly be.

I have felt this very strongly, for a long while—so strongly, in fact, in telling the story of the Virgin of Vieux, I began it in this way:

Quite naturally, we always associate Christmas with the birth of the Infant Jesus. But it seems to me that, in so doing, we sometimes leave the association incomplete. The story of the Nativity is not only the story of the Christ Child; it is also the story of the angels who formed the multitudes of the heavenly host and of the shepherds who watched their flocks by night. It is the story of a star—and of a stable; of a royal Scion—and of a fulfilled prophecy. Even more, it is the story of a carpenter's betrothed wife who became the Mother of God's only begotten Son. Like many other birthday stories, it is not told in its entirety if it is confined to rejoicing over a new-born baby, even though this Baby be the Prince of Peace and the Redeemer of the World; it must include a tribute to the Baby's Mother. . . .

Now I feel this more strongly than ever. I am very happy in making all the traditional preparations for the homecoming of my children and grandchildren who will soon be joining me here: in hanging wreaths, and trimming a tree and doing up presents and providing for the holiday feasts. And this year, when I arrange the crêche, I shall place the figures of the Wise Men far from the miniature stable at first, and then ask the children, every night at bedtime, to move them nearer and nearer, until on Twelfth Night they finally come close to the young Child and His Mother. This custom is not traditional with us; it is one I observed, with admiration, among the families I visited in Venezuela since we have had a Christmas at home. Now I am happy to introduce it into our own midst, for I believe it will make the Christmas story more real and vivid to the children of our family than it ever has been before. I think that when they sing their carols and recite the immortal passages from St. Luke, as they always do, they will understand these better than ever before; and little by little they will realize, with increasing poignancy, that the Christmas giving which makes their day so happy was inspired by the greatest gift of all.

For it is the children's day too, of course. I hope and believe that I have left nothing undone which will make it their happiest day of the year, and nothing that will help them understand why it should be thus. But, as I make these cheerful preparations, I find that my own gladness because I have come home for Christmas and because this homecoming will be shared by most of my family, is crowned by the consciousness that The Holy Mother is watching over me, as she has all my life, and that my picture of her is not just a possession, not just a representation, but a reminder and a symbol and a challenge.

—*The Oxbow,*
Newbury, Vt.

Follow a Star

We three Kings of Orient are . . .

"We Three Kings of Orient are,
Bearing gifts we traverse afar,
Field and fountain, moor and mountain,
Following yonder star."

I DO NOT KNOW WHY THE WORDS OF THIS OLD
song came to me, apparently out of the blue, one day
lately when I was motoring between Avila and
Madrid—a route which, throughout the summer and
autumn, I have been taking fairly frequently in connection with current work. Usually, when I am in
Spain, I spend a good deal of time at the Prado—to

my way of thinking, the finest picture gallery in the world; and the masterpieces of Velazquez, among them "The Adoration of the Magi," receive the greater part of my attention. But this year I have been working so intensively that there has been practically no sightseeing; and certainly there is nothing about the gaunt though majestic countryside through which I was passing, and which bears so little resemblance to what is generally considered "typically Spanish," that recalled the song to me. Actually, it is most closely associated in my mind, not with foreign travel, but with certain carols sung along Beacon Hill in Boston on Christmas Eve, and which are folk songs tinged with religious feeling, rather than hymns, strictly speaking. I would say that this one belonged in the same category with "I Saw Three Ships Come Sailing By," for instance, and I had not thought of either one since I last heard them sung by carolers, clustered around a doorway in Louisburg Square, which was white with snow that glistened under the candlelight. But it was the three kings and not the three ships that so suddenly and so unexpectedly came crowding into the forefront of my consciousness and that have insistently stayed there ever since.

I am glad that they have. I have always thought their story was charming, touching and symbolic, ever since it was first told to me by my wonderful grandmother who, like St. John of the Cross—with whom I have much more recently become acquainted —knew the Bible so thoroughly that she did not need to refer to the well-worn copy which had been her future husband's first gift to her, in order to quote from it at length. She made those three kings, their clothes and their camels, their long journeys and their precious gifts very vivid to me. I was interested in their travels, for my eagerness to become familiar with unknown regions was unslaked. However, as a child, it was the gifts of the three kings which intrigued me most. What wonderful presents those were! How much more exciting they must have been to Jesus and to His Mother than the presents that are usually brought to a baby! But what, exactly, did the Holy Family do with them? The gold would have been useful of course, for expenses during the Flight into Egypt. But even my grandmother could not explain the eventual use to which frankincense and myrrh were probably put. However, I felt sure that they must be the right sort of present, just as many of mine had proved to be, though I had at first seen in them the fulfillment of no immediate need or wish.

I still do not know just how the frankincense and myrrh were used, nor do I greatly care now. Like most elderly persons, I find that presents, except as symbols, do not mean as much to me as when I was young. I have traveled a good deal myself, and though some of this journeying has been delightful, much of it has been hard going. It is the fact that the Magi were following a star which has come to seem supremely important to me.

Practical people are apt to tell us that stargazing is a senseless pursuit. But how can you follow a star unless you first gaze at it? And if you do not follow a star, then what should you follow? We can be very literal about this and remind skeptics that all mariners and many overland travelers follow the stars with mathematical precision; or we can be less literal and recall the persons who, in a figurative sense, have discovered that, only by following their stars, have they achieved either material or spiritual success. They have nearly always met with derision, whether their way led over mountains, through fields and moors, or kept close to fountains. Their companions, who persisted in looking at the rough road which they were jointly treading, its pitfalls and obstructions, instead of glancing up at the heavens, have always tried to convince the stargazers that they were doomed to failure, even if they did not lose their sense of direction or fall exhausted by the roadside. But those who have persevered have had their eventual reward. They have found that the star they were following finally came to rest at the place they wanted to reach. And not a few of them have discovered that this place was glorified by the Presence of Christ Himself.

We cannot all take precious gifts with us to bestow where we would most like to do so as we journey through life, and this journey is apt to be marked by more mountains we must climb than fountains beside which we can rest. But we can all follow a star. And if we do so with faith as well as persistence, it will be no miracle if, at the end of the rough road, we find "The Young Child and His Mother." For that is part of the everlasting promise of Christmas, which has never been broken.

—*Palacete Montefrío,*
Avila, Spain.

The Author and Her Book

FRANCES PARKINSON KEYES, whose books have been best-sellers almost every year since 1936 and are published simul-taneously in England and the United States and in as many as twelve foreign languages, was born at the University of Virginia, where her father, John Henry Wheeler, a Bostonian transplanted to the South, was head of the Greek department. Her mother was Louise Fuller Johnson, a New Yorker who had earlier been transplanted to Newbury, Vermont. After Dr. Wheeler's death in Virginia, Frances and her mother spent their summers in Newbury and their winters in Boston, a city which was to become the scene of *Joy Street* (Messner, 1950), a best-seller of 1950-51. As a girl she studied in Geneva and Berlin, as well as Boston, and with a governess in the country—she speaks four languages—and even today spends much time in travel. She was married at eighteen to Henry Wilder Keyes, whose home, Pine Grove Farm, near Haver-hill, New Hampshire, was just across the river from New-bury, Vermont. In 1917 he became governor of New Hampshire. In 1919 he was elected to the United States Senate and served three terms, during which Mrs. Keyes divided her time between her family of three sons and the beginning of a literary career, initiated with articles in the Atlantic

Monthly and a novel, *The Old Gray Homestead* (Houghton Mifflin, 1919). Her interest in her husband's Washington career led her to depict Washington political life in a series of letters to American women which became a Good Housekeeping running feature entitled *The Letters from a Senator's Wife* and was later published in book form by Appleton in 1924. In 1923 she began a novel set in Washington which appeared in 1930 as *Queen Anne's Lace* (Liveright, 1930). From 1923 to 1935 she was an associate editor of Good Housekeeping and from 1937 to 1939 editor of the National Historical Magazine. Mrs. Keyes has spent much time in France, which led to the biography of St. Therese, *Written in Heaven* (Messner, 1937), and the life of St. Bernadette of Lourdes, *The Sublime Shepherdess* (Messner, 1940), and a more personal record, *Along a Little Way* (Messner, 1940). In 1940 she visited Mexico to write *The Grace of Guadalupe* (Messner, 1941). Mrs. Keyes holds degrees of Litt. D. from Bates College and George Washington University, and in 1951 received the degree of Doctor of Humane Letters from the University of New Hampshire "as a distinguished author, ambassador of good will, and interpreter of American life." In 1946 she received the Siena Medal awarded annually to "The outstanding Catholic woman in the United States"; in 1950 the Silver Medal of French Recognition for her aid in reconstructing the Abbaye of the Benedictines at Lisieux; and in 1959 she was decorated with the Order Of Isabella the Catholic for recognition of her work in Spain. She still retains her ownership of the Oxbow, her ancestral homestead at Newbury, Vermont, and her legal residence is still at Pine Grove Farm, the Keyes' family home at North Haverhill, New Hampshire; but in the winter she uses the historic Beauregard House, in New Orleans, which she has restored, as her writing center. Among her books besides those previously mentioned are: *The Career of David Noble* (Frederick Stokes, 1921), *Silver Seas and Golden Cities* (Liveright, 1931), *Lady Blanche Farm* (Liveright, 1931), *Senator Marlowe's Daughter* (Messner, 1933), *The Safe Bridge* (Messner, 1934), *The Happy Wanderer* (Messner, 1935), *Honor Bright* (Messner, 1936), *Capital Kaleidoscope* (1937), *Parts Unknown* (Messner, 1938), *The Great Tradition* (Messner, 1939), *Fielding's Folly* (Messner, 1940), *All that Glitters* (Messner, 1941), *Crescent Carnival* (Messner, 1942), *Also the Hills* (Messner, 1942), *The River Road* (Messner, 1945), *Once on Esplanade* (Dodd, Mead, 1947), *Came a Cavalier* (Messner, 1947), *Dinner at Antoine's* (Messner, 1948), *Therese: Saint of a Little Way* (Messner, 1950), *All This is Louisiana* (Harper Bros., 1950), *The Cost of a Best Seller* (Messner, 1950), *Steamboat Gothic* (Messner, 1952), *Bernadette of Lourdes* (Messner, 1953), *The Royal Box* (Messner, 1954), *The Frances Parkinson Keyes Cookbook* (Doubleday, 1955), *St. Anne: Grandmother of Our Saviour* (Messner, 1955), *Blue Camellia* (Messner, 1957), *The Land of Stones and Saints* (Doubleday, 1957), *Victorine* (Messner, 1958), *Station Wagon in Spain* (Farrar, Straus & Cudahy, 1959).

FRANCES PARKINSON KEYES' CHRISTMAS GIFT (Hawthorn, 1959) was designed by Marshall Lee and completely manufactured by the H. Wolff Book Manufacturing Company, New York. The body type is Granjon, designed for Linotype under the supervision of George W. Jones and named after the French type designer, Robert Granjon.